Silent Partners

Glimpses from Scripture

Claire Wilson

British Library Cataloguing in Publication Data:
a catalogue record for this publication
is available from the British Library

ISBN   978-1-912052-69-1

© Handsel Press

Typeset in 12 pt Minion Pro at Haddington, Scotland

Printed by West Port Print, St Andrews

Cover design by Margot Dunnachie
based on original artwork by Claire Wilson

Contents

Holy Mystery

There is a tacit silence,
a hidden understanding
that there are moments
too tender to witness,
too powerful not to –
places of holy mystery
that we shy away from
lest we also be observed;
lest the constriction of throat,
the welling of eye
betray that we feel something.

Is that why *You* say,
'Where are you?'
'Why are you hiding?'
when *You* want to walk with us
in the garden,
not eyeball to eyeball
but side by side
so that our gaze may rest
on a more distant horizon
and words and silence take shape
like a skein – taking turns to lead
or murmuration –
where it is impossible to spot
the pivot of such communion.

Yet God

Adam and Eve
driven out
yet God provides

Hagar
abandoned
yet God sees

Moses
murder flight
yet God appears

Prodigal son
wants father dead
yet father welcomes his return

Older brother
won't come in
yet father reaches out

Jesus
betrayed
yet God brings life

Even yet, God
provides
sees
appears
welcomes
reaches out
brings life

Leah

You are shortsighted
and don't see it coming
that this defect will mar
what's there in the offing:

Obstruct those romances
even blight marriage chances
that wait with the sheep
by the wells in the fields.

Such a flurry of fever
at Jacob's arrival
on the run from his brother,
a dark veil of mystery.

You join all the women
in hoping and teasing.
The heart-aching question is
who'll win his favour?

Custom and habit
mean you're in the running,
but it soon becomes clear
you'll be pipped at the post.

Even so, filled with fear,
and hidden by veils,
you are passed off as Rachel
– an all round betrayal.

The God of your husband
takes note of your weeping,
unloved as you are,
puts sons in your keeping

and, taking the long view,
ensures that a people,
a priesthood, a saviour
will come in due time.

Rachel's son, Joseph,
becomes the forerunner –
ensures that a nation
survives through a famine.

But your Judah's line
will lead to a Saviour,
bring sight to the blind
and light to all people.

Potiphar's Wife

I shall remain nameless
but not blameless
for my story has a frame
that does nothing
to enhance my reputation

I was married young
to an older man.
Was my 'high official' husband
impotent – no fun for me
and no threat
to those who placed him in authority?

Or was it me
who could not produce
the requisite proof
that this relationship was viable?

Or was he gay,
eyeing that young foreigner
bringing him here as slave,
grooming him, teasing
with responsibility,
setting him up to fall
for our amusement?

Or was he to be
the prize bull
bringing progeny
with my complicity?

Whatever the back story,
with the master so often away,
the childbearing years
soon to pass,

whatever looks I'd had fading
and this specimen passing
before my eyes each day —
what was a woman to do?
Infatuation grew
not to name frustration

And when the moment came
and passed
with his claim of loyalty
to his master and his God,
his cloak was his downfall
left in my hand.

Easy enough to fake the news
rehearsed on servants,
recounted in earnest
for the master's ears
with a little twist of blame
for it was his fault
for bringing the Hebrew here
in the first place.

But why, when death
should be the penalty,
was jail deemed enough?
Did Potiphar not take me at my word?
Was he also blinded by that beauty
or not fooled by that pinch of salt?

As I said,
with a reputation to protect,
I am not blameless
but shall remain nameless.

Bathsheba

Had he eyed you up awhile
before summoning you in,
or was it just an opportunist,
spur of the moment thing?

When rape led on to murder
of a decent, well loved man –
when the king had got you pregnant
what on earth did you feel then?

Was guilt piled on betrayal?
It's somehow now your fault –
bathing outside, flaunting beauty –
mentioning the month without . . .

He confesses to that God of his
(Nathan's story ringing),
"Against God only have I sinned."
He feels a psalm beginning.

But your name is made public,
dragged through mud for all of time.
Did his repentance touch you?
Do chattels hold their stain?

Nine long months you mourned that foray,
that invasion, in the spring
when kings go out to battle,
falsehood growing, ripening

in the shameful, hidden place
while he, behind the lines,
was free to find his comfort
in his concubines and wives.

Or was he devastated too,
though riding high above it all,
that slight transgression of the eye
could result in such a fall?

Did he join your desolation
after birth while yet defiled,
still hoping God might change his mind,
commuting sentence on the child?

And when Solomon was born,
was heart as well as womb the dust
in which he grew, a home for love
and not just dominating lust?

The echo of another voice
hints hope of something more,
to change the earth, to cradle
a much wiser king. Look for

one who goes the long way round
to meet a woman face to face
beside a well for conversation
disabusing all disgrace.

Died in Infancy

There probably is no memorial stone.
Who knows of the customs back then
even, as here, for a mighty king's son?
Much less likely, the bastard wean.

Yet, millennia on, you still hear about me,
nameless note at the end of a page,
an inconvenient truth magnified
by my sire's guilty grief, sin and rage.

Nothing is said about my mother's pain
but God knew me right from the start;
knit me together in Bathsheba's womb
beheld who I am in God's heart.

My seven days appear in God's book,
all envisaged before there was one
cradled close to her breast until summoned home
leaving him, her and you one question.

Can meaning be hidden in some preacher's tale
or is this more than we can descry?
Who is this God who has someone so small
bear such weight; who has God's own son die?

Advent Questions

Something about not knowing,
an anxiety that gnaws at patience,
a niggle that leaves a question hanging.

In that last month or so,
when the census was called,
with that chance to escape scrutiny,
were you lonely, Mary,
despite the lumbering companionship
of that older man?

Did you wonder where you might be
on the Big Day?
Whether someone would have room
to include you?
While you played hostess to a surprise guest,
could you ever have guessed
at the questions he would bring to the world
each Christmas?

How many prospective guests today
live out your hanging questions . . .

Teach us, Mary, when we host
the one you bore in such tiny form,
to watch our tread
maybe let in angels, unaware.

Parenting

You were carrying out your role,
the high point of your career,
very much in the public eye
and probably anxious
to fulfil every requirement.
Although this took you
into the most sacred place
I doubt it occurred to you
that the Almighty was waiting
to meet you
in the most painful longing of your soul.
So you were dumbstruck
and hobbled through the rest of your term
until you could get home.

And was Elizabeth confounded
to see the state you were in?
And did she show you tenderness,
absent for some time
after the monthly disappointments
and unmentioned shadow
of that shameful empty womb.

No wonder she took herself off
lest others imagine what you'd been up to
in some unexpected night of passion.
And was it something like it
that brought young Mary to her side
but which lead to leaping hearts
and such a song
that echoes down the years.

There was a hullabaloo
about the naming –
rumour, gossip, innuendo.
Did the cousins share their boyhood,
compare notes?
Or laugh about wrong footing adults
in that adventure in the temple
or put the world to rights
with adolescent fervour
before going their own ways
into desert and carpentry?

John, did your parents tear their hair out
when you headed into lonely places,
turned into a wild man
with your locusts and honey?
Maybe they spoke with Mary
about that washing in the Jordan
that was accompanied by thunder.
I keep hoping
that they didn't live to hear
about you losing your head.

You Had no Womb

You had no womb
but you knew one from within
learning to kick and turn
suck and squirm
push against constraint.

From heaven's cocoon
you dawned
from and in
fragile flesh and skin
just as we did

At the mercy of first timers
making each faux pas
with no Mothercare
or grandmother to dandle
and dawdle with.

Who were the unnamed friends
and strangers who sheltered you
and them in exile
returning the long way round
to home you'd never seen?

You may not have known first hand
the 'issues of blood'
but you were at close quarters
with mother and sisters,
their heralds of fret and pain
proclaiming, 'unclean,' back then.

No doubt there was nonsense
to sift from fact
in your adolescent brain
but we know you knew
the need to run away
(or at least stay behind)
choose your own way

Then submit again
to the slow,
soul speed,
coming into your own -
that came to such grief and glory
in the end.

The Silent Partner

I was harassed.
He'd gone with his fishing mates
to hear the preacher -
after all, it was the Sabbath.
I was at home, trying to 'not work.'
Does quelling a fever count?
Does fielding a toddler?
Does laying down the law to local lads
about their racket and their mess?

Anyway, the next thing I know
Peter's back
with not just James and John
but the joiner as well,
looking for food,
eyes aglow.
I can't believe he'd be so thoughtless.

I manage a whispered exchange,
explain about Mum,
try to keep the wee one out of her room
and only enough prepared for the family
. . . but . . .

'You should have seen what happened in there –
everyone was amazed!
He put demons out –
as well as noses!
Look, I invited him; he's here now.
Maybe the touch hasn't left him yet.
Let's ask him to do something for your Mum.'

There's no scope for argument.

He glances over, gets up,
crosses the room
and, chucking the wee one under the chin,
bids me lead the way.

'These things happen,' he says to Peter
while I'm tidying as I go ahead,
'It's ok. I've lived at home. I know what it's like.'

I show him to her room.
I'm watching through the crack.
Standing by her bed, his back to me
he bids the fever leave –
not just from her but from the house as well.
I breathe a sigh –
a poorly child is hell.
He kneels beside her, whispering,
inviting her to serve.

Turning, he tells me to help her up, but,
'Take all the time you need.'
He takes the child from my hip.
'I've got some fun to have with this wee man. We'll wait.'

It all comes together – the meal, I mean,
and somehow seals a deal for us
to let Peter do what he has to do
in the coming weeks, months, years.

Starlit, the crowds gather
in our yard, no less.
He greets them one by one –
each leaving 'well,' in extraordinary ways.

He can't have had more than a few hours sleep.
It was still going on when I went to bed,
happy but overwhelmed at day's end.

Rising early,
the sky red with dawn,
I notice him already at prayer.
Returning with water
the wee one's playing at his feet
while Mum bustles about
getting breakfast together
and a piece for later.
It isn't right for me to speak with him
before Peter's up
but it is comfortable
hearing him murmur with the child
while Mum and I whisper together.

. . . .

I think you know my thoughts:
you know what it is like
to have people appreciating you,
demanding from you,
clinging to you
when you know there is more,
something different for you to do as well.

Show me what it means to be your partner.

The Path Ahead

You've just outlined the path ahead
a scary prospect
but yours to tread.

A mother comes
and kneels;
perceives you have the power,
finds it possible to ask
what is impossible.

What does she hear
in that exchange?
Her ambition rebuked
or her sons' assertion –
misguided, rash,
but translated:
'You will indeed drink my cup.'

'You will indeed
taste challenge
   the like of which you have never seen,
swallow separation
   from all that is dear
drain life so deeply
   it will be a miracle
should you ever burst free.

The path ahead
is one of serving,
giving,
laying down,
paying forward . . .
a different kind of wishing to be great.

The Blanket

In one version,
in my mind's eye,
Jesus holds their gaze
as he makes that statement,
'Which is easier to say . . .'

And as the man gets to his feet,
testing unused muscles
and balance
and hope,
Jesus folds the blanket
or bedroll
or whatever it was
and hands it to him
as a parting bonus.

There is a song
about wartime,
though it could be about
other lonely
or challenging times,
that ends,
'we wrap ourselves in prayer.'

Was that blanket
woven of the prayers
and hospitality
of friends?

When he got home,
did the man
sometimes get it out
and wrap himself round
letting protection and warmth
remind him
of a touchstone moment?

Or might he, one day,
wrap it round his child
or pass it on
to someone
whose need is greater?

The Storm

Some are stripped for rowing,
others clutch their windblown clothes
or hang on to a rope
for dear life.

Jesus sleeps
as does John close by.

One has lost his oar,
another tries in vain to steer
looking behind rather than ahead,
another holds up his hands in horror.

Which of the others am I?
One of those still trying to row,
making little difference
but feeling better for trying?
Or maybe following an instinct
to keep doing
'What is in my hand?'

Is my oar in mid pull
or at the turn
to lift through spray?
Is the sea tossed like rapids and,
in trying to keep a rhythm
does water crash my lifted oar,
that pulls again
on empty air?

I'm tempted
to a faster stroke
or should I watch
and wait
and match the dip
to rolling wave?

Lord, your peaceful rest
about to be disturbed again:
I need to feel you, see you
piloting our boat
in charge.

WAKE UP!

Mary's Friday

My son, my son,
Why have you forsaken me?
Why did my, 'Yes,'
so long ago
arrive here,
at a place riven
with anguish?
How can it be
that friends who followed, surrounded you
are nowhere to be seen?
Why does the enemy have the upper hand?

And yet, before the end,
you call another son
to be soul friend;
call me to be at home
with him, with them,
the many daughters, sons
of faith,
of hope,
of love
and so to find
you there
again.

Easter Saturday

Some of us scattered
after the arrest –
barely able to look
one another in the eye
but unable to be alone
either,
unable to articulate
anything
of this inconceivable thing
that was happening.

Suddenly, events tumbled
guts churned
rumours swirled
as did we amongst onlookers,
strangers,
visitors who knew nothing,
faces recognised
from one miracle or another.

After the cry,
'It is done!'
What was there to do
but sit red-eyed, or
toss and turn and weep and rail
at the fools we had become?

We who had chosen to follow;
we who had cast in our lot;
had snatched it back again,
unable, after all,
to go right to the end.

From Advent to Easter

You grew into yourself
awkward guest
surprising host . . .
yourself

Wine from well water,
health for sick mother
(who then cooks your dinner)
questioning manners,
provoking largesse
(in a taxman, no less.)

Tales for one sister
fluster a hostess
at all the unfairness.
You embarrass your host
at that stingy man's junket –
a fragrance, a sweetness
that floozy brings in!

Turn picnic to banquet;
stun traitor and friends
by washing their feet,
not their hands,
at Passover time
before they can eat.

In the end, so it seems,
the rule book tossed over,
you upset enough people
that they take the matter
in their unwashed hands,
hoisting you higher
on your own petard.

Even so, just days later
you are spotted abroad
honoured guest breaking bread
and as host, cooking breakfast -
grilled fish by the water —
now more than ever yourself.

Life

Today,
the path is strewn
with gold:
here pooled,
a mirror
for the thinning,
crown above;
there, a breath
animates
both loosened leaf
that drifts to earth
and settled pile
that thought this
was the final resting place.

Above the ground
we miss the life
that pulses through
the mystery of soil
and leaches out
into our veins –
all that nourished us,
let us unfurl
dance in breeze
and weather countless storms
till our new colours
heralded this fall.

Who knows
what our new dress will be?
Yet Christ,
our stamping ground,
both paved
and walked the way,
wants us to know
his company
into eternity.

This Bench

This bench just waiting
by your path may overhear
a sacred moment

There is room for three
on this bench: your voice and mine
and Spirit whisper

Space on this bench here –
wait, notice, really hear, see
where life is calling

Sit awhile and share.
This bench will bear your weight till
melody rings clear

*With thanks both for and to the many companions
on this journey. You know who you are.*